Low Sodium Meal Prep Cookbook for Beginners

800-Day Prep-and-Go Low-Sodium Recipes with No-Stress Meal Plans to Lower Blood Pressure and Improve Your Health

Fekam Slety

© Copyright 2021 Fekam Slety - All Rights Reserved.

In no way is it legal to reproduce, duplicate, or transmit any part of this document by either electronic means or in printed format. Recording of this publication is strictly prohibited, and any storage of this material is not allowed unless with written permission from the publisher. All rights reserved.

The information provided herein is stated to be truthful and consistent, in that any liability, regarding inattention or otherwise, by any usage or abuse of any policies, processes, or directions contained within is the solitary and complete responsibility of the recipient reader. Under no circumstances will any legal liability or blame be held against the publisher for any reparation, damages, or monetary loss due to the information herein, either directly or indirectly.

Respective authors own all copyrights not held by the publisher.

Legal Notice:

This book is copyright protected. This is only for personal use. You cannot amend, distribute, sell, use, quote or paraphrase any part of the content within this book without the consent of the author or copyright owner. Legal action will be pursued if this is breached.

Disclaimer Notice:

Please note the information contained within this document is for educational and entertainment purposes only. Every attempt has been made to provide accurate, up-to-date and reliable, complete information. No warranties of any kind are expressed or implied. Readers acknowledge that the author is not engaging in the rendering of legal, financial, medical or professional advice.

By reading this document, the reader agrees that under no circumstances are we responsible for any losses, direct or indirect, which are incurred as a result of the use of information contained within this document, including, but not limited to, errors, omissions, or inaccuracies.

Table of Contents

Introduction 7
Chapter 1: Overview of Low Sodium Diet **8**
    Where Diet And Health Intersect 8
    About Sodium 8
    The Truth About Sea Salt and Salt Replacements 10
    Understanding Your Diagnosis: High Blood Pressure 10
    Benefits of Plant-Based Die Understanding Your Diagnosis: Heart Disease 11
    Menière's disease 14
    Considering Potassium 15
    The Challenge and the Solution 16
Chapter 2: Why Meal Prep? **17**
    The Common Mistakes by Meal Prepping Beginners 17
    The Benefits of Meal Prep 17
Chapter 3: 30-Day Meal Plan **19**
Chapter 4: Breakfast Recipes **25**
    Hash Browns 25
    Breakfast Sausage 26
    Breakfast Biscuits 27
    Flaxseed French Toast with Strawberries 28
    Breakfast Casserole 29
    Egg Tarts 30
    Broccoli & Cheese Quiche 31
    Breakfast Peppers 32
    Cheesy Frittata 33
    Breakfast Stuffed Pastries 34

Chapter 5: Chicken Recipes **35**

    Crunchy Chicken Tenderloins 35

    Chicken & Broccoli 36

    Mexican Chicken Wings 37

    Crispy Chicken Breast 38

    General Tso's Chicken 39

    Buttermilk Fried Chicken 41

    Parmesan Chicken 43

    Korean Fried Chicken 44

    Lemon Chicken 46

    Roast Chicken 47

Chapter 6: Meat Recipes **48**

    Ranch Pork Chops 48

    Rib Eye Steak 49

    Meatballs 50

    Sausages 51

    Roast Beef 52

    Mustard Pork Tenderloin 53

    Pork Chops & Brussels Sprouts 54

    Garlic & Rosemary Lamb Chops 55

    Juicy Steaks 56

    Lamb Chops with Mustard & Garlic 57

Chapter 7: Fish & Seafood Recipes **58**

    Scallops with Lemon Herb Sauce 58

    Sesame Cod & Snap Peas 59

    Coconut Shrimp 60

    Calamari 62

Crispy Fish 63

Garlic Popcorn Shrimp 64

Salmon with Horseradish Rub 66

Lemon Paprika Shrimp 67

Salmon Cakes with Spicy Mayo 68

Fish Cakes 69

Chapter 8: Vegetarian Recipes **70**

Eggplant Parmesan 70

Falafel 72

Brussels Sprouts with Bacon 73

Baked Potatoes with Broccoli 74

Roasted Okra 75

Crispy Green Tomatoes 76

Onion Rings 77

Spicy Green Beans 78

Baked Potatoes 79

Roasted Vegetables 80

Chapter 9: Snack Recipes **81**

Fish & Chips 81

Spicy Potato Wedges 83

Curried Chickpeas 84

Sesame Kale Chips 85

Cinnamon Plantain Chips 86

Potato Chips 87

Greek Feta Fries 88

Zucchini Chips 90

Pickle Chips 92

Roasted Peanuts 93

Chapter 10: Appetizer Recipes **94**

Buffalo Wings 94

Stuffed Peppers 96

Egg Rolls 97

Mac & Cheese Balls 98

Pork Dumplings 99

Jalapeño Poppers 101

Scallops with Bacon 102

Peppers Stuffed with Sausage 103

Tofu Bites 104

Sausage Bites 105

Chapter 10: Side Dish Recipes **106**

Roasted Cauliflower & Broccoli 106

Cauliflower Gnocchi 107

Orange & Sesame Tofu 108

Garlic Baby Potatoes 109

Roasted Butternut Squash 110

Conclusion **111**

Introduction

Here's a low sodium cookbook that can actually help you to plan out your whole day's meals. This low sodium diet can help you out with handy advice for managing your salt intake, provide effective shopping tips and helpful cooking tips, and provide convenient advice.

This cookbook provides beginners with a detailed 30-day meal plan, including low sodium diet breakfast, low sodium diet lunch and low sodium diet dinner recipes, which can help people control the rise of blood pressure and keep fit.

This Low Sodium Meal Prep Cookbook for Beginners will allow you to find foods easier, you not only can eat more balanced and nutritious, but also can have tasty meals at home without much effort.

Chapter 1: Overview of Low Sodium Diet

Where Diet And Health Intersect

If you are reading this, you've probably been told that, for health reasons, you need to reduce the amount of sodium in your diet. Maybe you have been diagnosed with one of the many conditions where you would benefit from a low-sodium diet, such as high blood pressure, heart disease, kidney disease, liver disease, Manière's disease, or another condition.

You may have been surprised by your diagnosis, and you may still be in shock or denial, but now you are asking yourself: How do I start a low sodium diet? My own journey to a low-sodium diet began with cardiac disease and high blood pressure, so I understand what you are going through and I'm here to help.

Sodium is a major contributor to high blood pressure, and many Americans unwittingly consume up to 20 times more sodium than their body needs each day. In this chapter, we will examine sodium, the unexpected places where it is found in our diets, and how to limit sodium consumption in an effort to live longer, healthier lives.

About Sodium

Sodium chloride (NACL), or salt, is an electrolyte (an electrically conducting solution when dissolved in water) that is an essential part of our physical makeup, allowing our bodies to function optimally. Sodium balances the body's fluid levels, allows for the transmission of signals from nerves, aids our muscles in movement, and helps with digestion.

However, like all the other electrolytes in our bodies (potassium, calcium, magnesium, bicarbonate, chloride, and hydrogen phosphate), salt must be maintained within a certain healthy level. Extremely low sodium is as dangerous as extremely high sodium. If your body has extremely low sodium, your heart may not generate the electricity needed to make it beat, or it may cause your heart to go into a rapid heartbeat that could be dangerous. High sodium, over time, leads to hypertension, which can damage the veins, arteries, kidneys, and heart. That can lead to further heart disease. Therefore, it's important to consult your physician to determine the proper salt balance for you.

Sodium makes our bodies draw extra water into our blood vessels and increases the blood volume in our arteries and veins, which can cause high blood pressure. Heart.org likens it to "turning up the supply in a garden hose." If a high level of sodium continues to remain in the blood stream, our blood vessels can become permanently stretched and strained. It is this damage, weakness, and inflexibility (you may have heard the phrase "hardening of the arteries") that leads to heart attacks later in life.

If your doctor has determined that you should begin controlling your sodium levels, he or she more than likely also gave you a daily limit of grams or milligrams of sodium. If not, ask your practitioner for a specific number to aim for before beginning a low-sodium diet.

The United States Department of Agriculture (USDA) recommends 2,300 milligrams (mg) of sodium per day for a healthy person without high blood pressure or heart disease. The American Heart Association (AHA) recommends 1,500mg per day. Recently, the Mayo Clinic recommended 1,500mg of sodium per day for all Americans aged 51 and above. (The disparity between the USDA and AHA and Mayo Clinic is because the USDA has not reviewed their recommendations recently, whereas the other two organizations review medical research and findings regularly.) The problem is, most Americans consume 3,000 to 6,000mg of sodium on a daily basis.

You may think: Okay, 1,500mg or less a day doesn't sound too bad. I can do that. But what does that really look like? It's surprising how little 1,500mg of sodium actually amounts to: It is equal to 3/4 teaspoon of salt. You read that correctly-LESS than ONE teaspoon. But I behave; I rarely use the salt shaker to add extra salt on my food! Unfortunately, most of the sodium we consume comes from the processed foods we eat. Sodium is everywhere-in baked goods, cheeses, deli meats, sauces-almost everything we purchase.

But never fear! It is possible to enjoy your food on 1,500mg of sodium per day. By using this book as a guide to create a healthy low-sodium lifestyle, you can start taking action immediately to lower your risk-or the risk of someone you love-of having a first (or subsequent) heart attack(s). Together, we will discover some new skills to succeed at living a lows, odium life. Learning how to effectively read and understand food labels, and becoming accustomed to cooking healthy food at home will be the two most beneficial skills you can acquire and improve upon.

The Truth About Sea Salt and Salt Replacements

Salt is salt is salt. At its molecular core, it is all Sodium Chloride (NaCl). Sea salt may have a better taste or trace minerals that may be good for you, but it is still salt. It comes with fancy names on packages: Fleur de Sel, Celtic Gray, Himalayan, Pink Hawaiian, and so on, but it is still detrimental to your health in quantities above 1,500mg a day.

Most salt replacements use potassium chloride. Potassium chloride must be avoided by heart, liver, and kidney patients, as it interacts negatively with most of the medicines used to treat those conditions (such as aspirin, Coumadin, Lasix [furosemide, metoprolol], Plavix, antirejection medications [Tacrolimus, sirolimus, mycophenolate], vitamin B12, and Lantus). For those who have had heart transplants, like me, and regularly take those medications, it's especially challenging to make sure that any low-sodium items used are truly low in sodium and do not use potassium chloride as a replacement for salt.

Understanding Your Diagnosis: High Blood Pressure

Unless your doctor has already diagnosed you with high blood pressure, you may not have a clear idea of what constitutes "good" blood pressure versus "bad." Simply put, having high blood pressure means that your heart has to work harder to pump blood through your body, and this extra work puts excess pressure on your arteries, which creates tension that makes it that much harder for your heart to do its job.

When you visit your doctor's office for a blood pressure reading, the doctor logs two numbers:

- **Systolic**

(the top/"over" number) indicates how much pressure your blood is exerting against your artery walls when the heart beats.

- **Diastolic**

(the lower number) indicates how much pressure your blood is exerting against your artery walls while the heart is at rest between beats.

While having a higher than normal reading for either number isn't ideal (see the following chart for your target blood pressure range), it is usually the top, or systolic number that is considered more important. The latest research shows that the systolic blood pressure gives the best indication of your risk of having a stroke or heart attack.

What causes high blood pressure? Essential (primary) hypertension has no known cause. It gradually develops over time. Secondary hypertension is caused by other conditions such as kidney disease, some birth control pills, sleep apnea, and more.

The scariest part about high blood pressure is that while it can do so much damage, it typically has no signs or symptoms-one out of every five people with high blood pressure don't even know they have it. The only way to know whether you're in the normal range or have high blood pressure is to get checked regularly.

There is no cure for high blood pressure, but it can be controlled. You must consistently monitor your blood pressure and manage it through sensible lifestyle changes such as a low sodium diet, regular exercise, and ceasing smoking. (Always consult your doctor before beginning a lifestyle change, and to determine your optimal blood pressure numbers.)

Improving your diet and maintaining your sodium can provide noticeable health benefits in a short time. You should have less water retention and bloating as you reduce the levels of sodium you intake. Carrying less water weight means the heart doesn't have to work as hard to push the blood through your body. If you tend to carry water weight in your abdomen, then less water retention in that area means that the weight of that water isn't impairing your lungs and breathing. It will also reduce the workload of the kidneys, and improved blood flow to the kidneys can allow for even less water retention.

Benefits of Plant-Based Die Understanding Your Diagnosis: Heart Disease

Heart disease is the leading cause of death for both men and women in the United States. It can occur at any age, however. In the United States, four out of five people who die from coronary heart disease are aged 65 or older.

According to the National Institute of Health (NIH), "Coronary heart disease-often simply called heart disease-is the main form of heart disease. It is a disorder of the blood vessels of the heart that can lead to heart attack. A heart attack happens when an artery becomes blocked, preventing oxygen and nutrients from getting to the heart. Heart disease is one of several cardiovascular diseases, which are diseases of the heart and blood vessel system. Other cardiovascular diseases include stroke, high blood pressure, angina (chest pain), and rheumatic heart disease."

Sadly, due to the lack of attention some people place on the health of their hearts, many people are diagnosed only after they have experienced a major heart episode, such as a heart attack or stroke. Your primary doctor diagnoses coronary heart disease (CHD) based on your medical and family histories, your risk factors, a physical exam, and the results from tests and procedures. If your primary doctor does not have experience, or if your case is serious, you may be referred to a cardiologist.

There are several tests to determine your risk, whether or not you have CHD, and if you do, at what stage of CHD you are currently at. Some of the tests are (for more in-depth descriptions, visit the National Institutes of Health online):

- **EKG (Electrocardiogram)**

An EKG detects and records the heart's electrical activity.

- **Stress Testing**

During stress testing, you exercise to make your heart work hard and beat fast while heart tests are done.

- **Echocardiography**

Echocardiography (or echo) uses sound waves to create a moving picture of your heart. The test provides information about the size and shape of your heart and how well your heart chambers and valves are working.

- **Chest X-ray**

A chest X-ray can reveal signs of heart failure, as well as lung disorders and other causes of symptoms not related to CHD.

- **Blood Tests**

Blood tests check the levels of certain fats, cholesterol, sugar, and proteins in your blood. Abnormal levels may be a sign that you're at risk. Blood tests also help detect anemia, a risk factor for CHD.

- **Coronary Angiography and Cardiac Catheterization**

Your doctor may recommend coronary angiography if other tests or factors suggest you have CHD. This test uses dye and special X-rays to look inside your coronary arteries.

What are the risk factors for heart disease? The following risk factors don't automatically mean you have CHD, but they all contribute to the probability you may contract CHD without changing your habits and lifestyle:

- High blood pressure
- High blood cholesterol
- Diabetes and prediabetes
- Smoking
- Being overweight or obese
- Being physically inactive
- Having a family history of early heart disease
- Having a history of preeclampsia during pregnancy
- Unhealthy diet
- Age (50 or older for men and women. Those of African-American descent have even greater risk factors)

Cardiovascular disease symptoms may be different for men and women. For instance, men are more likely to have chest pain; women are more likely to have symptoms such as shortness of breath, nausea, and extreme fatigue.

Symptoms for men and women can include:

- Chest pain (angina)
- Shortness of breath
- Pain, numbness, weakness, or coldness in your legs or arms if the blood vessels in those parts of your body are narrowed
- Pain in the neck, jaw, throat, upper abdomen, or back
- Fluttering in your chest
- Racing heartbeat (tachycardia)
- Slow heartbeat (bradycardia)

- Chest pain or discomfort
- Lightheadedness
- Dizziness
- Fainting (syncope) or near fainting
- Breathlessness with exertion or at rest
- Swelling of the legs, ankles, and feet
- Fatigue

Reducing sodium and improving your diet can ease your symptoms as they do for high blood pressure sufferers. You should see less water retention and bloating as you reduce the levels of sodium, which allows your heart to not work as hard.

Menière's disease

In the late 1800s at the Institute for Deaf-Mutes, French physician Prosper Menière concentrated his studies on a condition that combined hearing loss, tinnitus (or "ringing in the ear"), and vertigo (or dizziness), which was named in his honor as "Menière's Disease." While an exact cause for Menière's disease hasn't been specifically determined, one common result of the unnerving disorder is an accumulation of fluid in the inner ear.
Contributing factors to the disease could be heredity, allergies, head trauma, migraines, the result of an infection, or a combination of these factors.
As in all other parts of the human body, salt can also cause fluid accumulation in the inner ear. By limiting sodium intake and spacing intake throughout the day, you can help your body manage and process sodium more effectively. (Although the meal plans in the book don't explicitly address Menière's Disease, they can still be followed to help ease symptoms.) While there is no cure for Menière's Disease, limiting salt, not smoking, avoiding caffeine and alcohol, and reducing stress have all been shown to help cope with and reduce attacks.
If symptoms are more severe, medications to quell the dizziness and shorten the length of attacks are available, as are antibiotic or corticosteroid injections into the middle ear to lessen vertigo.
Some patients find value in having short bursts of air delivered through an "air pulse

generator" (a tube placed in the ear drum), an endolymphatic shunt (or tube) implanted to drain fluid from the ear, or other more in-depth inner ear surgeries depending on the severity of the patient's symptoms.

If you think that you may have Menière's Disease, please check with your doctor or physician immediately, who can provide additional information and help you manage your condition.

Considering Potassium

Potassium helps counteract the effects of sodium-it relaxes blood vessels, thus lowering blood pressure, and helps remove sodium through the urine.

Most Americans do not reach the recommended daily allowance, but before going overboard, it's important to note that too much potassium can damage the kidneys.

To boost potassium in your diet, add foods such as bananas, beans, sweet potatoes, and tomatoes. Proponents of the National Institutes of Health DASH (Dietary Approaches to Stop Hypertension) Diet (dashdiet.org) developed a low-sodium diet high in fruits and vegetables, lean meats, low-fat and nonfat dairy, and whole grains-all foods naturally high in potassium.

Some medications, such as diuretics in the aldactone family, preserve levels of potassium. Do not increase potassium in your diet if you are on these medications. Avoid foods that have ingredients labeled potassium or K, KCL, or K+-the chemical symbols for potassium and related compounds.

Health Harvard offers these additional helpful tips if you are looking to lower the amount of potassium in your diet:

- Soak or boil vegetables and fruits to leach out some potassium.
- Avoid canned, salted, pickled, corned, spiced, and smoked meat and fish.
- Avoid imitation meat products containing soy or vegetable protein.
- Limit high-potassium fruits such as bananas, citrus fruits, and avocados.
- Avoid baked potatoes and baked acorn and butternut squash.
- Avoid all types of peas and beans, which are naturally high in potassium.

Some salt substitutes will also be very high in potassium, so be sure to carefully check the label before you purchase or liberally apply to your food.

The Challenge and the Solution

When adopting a low-sodium diet, the USDA goal is to consume less than 2,300mg of sodium a day. For the plan in this book, we use the Mayo Clinic's goal of 1,500mg a day. Sodium is absolutely everywhere, even in places you think it can't possibly be, such as breakfast cereal, breads, and "all natural" frozen chicken: the birds (even organically raised fliers) are pumped full of salt water prior to freezing to enhance appearance and-surprise-taste. So, really, it's difficult to ditch salt when it imparts a lot of the flavor we're used to.

One of the tools I found most helpful was learning to substitute spices for salt. I live in Minnesota, and here we often joke about how black pepper is considered a "spice." I promise we will venture beyond black pepper and Mrs. Dash in the spice department.

If there are other vitamins or minerals that can interfere with your health, we will do our best to address them; however, and I simply cannot stress this enough: This book is not intended to be a substitute for a medical diagnosis. Before starting any diet or medical plan, please consult your doctor or physician.

This book will help you relearn to cook, guide you in finding substitutions (including kitchen staples and condiments), and help you enjoy your way to a low-sodium diet.

Chapter 2: Why Meal Prep?

The Common Mistakes by Meal Prepping Beginners

Below, you'll find a list of the common mistakes committed by meal prep beginners. Make sure that you avoid these mistakes as much as possible.

Mistake # 1 – Not planning ahead

Cramming is never a good idea for meal preparation. The purpose of meal preparation is to save time and energy. But for you to achieve this, you need to prepare your meals in advance. If you do everything at the last minute, you'll end up sacrificing the quality of your dishes. You also end up getting stressed. Make sure that you set aside enough time and that you plan your meals carefully so that everything goes as smoothly as you'd want it to.

Mistake # 2 – Not doing an inventory of what you have in the kitchen

Do not make the mistake of ignoring the food that you already have in your kitchen. If you already have tomato sauce and you don't know that, you'll end up buying one at the grocery store. The result is food waste and extra unnecessary expenses. See to it that you check first what you have in your kitchen pantry and refrigerator so you can save money and you don't waste any food.

Mistake # 3 – Over preparation

You don't have to prepare for two to three months ahead! Meal prep is for preparing meals in advance but this does not mean that you have to prepare for many months. This will result in decline in the quality and taste of food. You don't want to store your meals that long. You can prepare meals in advance for a few days to one or two weeks.

Mistake # 4 – Taking it too seriously

Meal prep is supposed to be fun and worthwhile. If you feel that this is a chore, you might not end up cooking delicious meals. Make an effort to see the fun in meal prep. This way, you'll enjoy it and have more fun doing it.

The Benefits of Meal Prep

Here are the many benefits to meal preparation:

Benefit # 1 – Healthier choices

Whenever you prepare your meals in advance, it means that you plan your menu. And when you plan your menu, you can easily make the healthier choices. It's easier to make conscious efforts in the ingredients that you will use and go for those that will benefit your health more.
But when you are pressed for time, and you don't plan your meals, there's a bigger chance to end up choosing unhealthy dishes to eat because you don't have time to think.

Benefit # 2 – Time saver

Meal prep can save you a great deal of time. You just have to do the meal preparation one time, and then when it's time to eat, you simply have to reheat the food or do minimal cooking.
This is ideal particularly for those who do not have the luxury of time to prepare elaborate meals in the kitchen.

Benefit # 3 – Less stress

You'll find this benefit worthwhile. Meal prep can definitely reduce the stress and anxiety that you have each time you have to worry about what to serve to your family.
Now that you know all about meal prep benefits and tips for success, it's time to actually get started.

Chapter 3: 30-Day Meal Plan

Day 1

Breakfast: Crispy frittata

Lunch: Spicy green beans

Dinner: General Tso's chicken

Day 2

Breakfast: Breakfast peppers

Lunch: Crispy green tomatoes

Dinner: Sesame cod & snap peas

Day 3

Breakfast: Broccoli & cheese quiche

Lunch: Onion rings

Dinner: Salmon with horseradish rub

Day 4

Breakfast: Hash browns

Lunch: Coconut shrimp

Dinner: Salmon cakes with spicy mayo

Day 5

Breakfast: Egg tarts

Lunch: Roasted vegetables

Dinner: Garlic & rosemary lamb chops

Day 6

Breakfast: Breakfast biscuits

Lunch: Buttermilk fried chicken

Dinner: Garlic popcorn shrimp

Day 7

Breakfast: Breakfast sausage

Lunch: Chicken & broccoli

Dinner: Meatballs

Day 8

Breakfast: Breakfast sausage

Lunch: Crunchy chicken tenderloins

Dinner: Juicy steaks

Day 9

Breakfast: Flaxseed French toast with strawberries

Lunch: Korean fried chicken

Dinner: Sesame cod & snap peas

Day 10

Breakfast: Breakfast peppers

Lunch: Crispy fish

Dinner: Mustard pork tenderloin

Day 11

Breakfast: Broccoli & cheese quiche

Lunch: Roasted okra

Dinner: Garlic popcorn shrimp

Day 12

Breakfast: Breakfast casserole

Lunch: Brussels sprouts with bacon

Dinner: Lemon chicken

Day 13

Breakfast: Hash Browns

Lunch: Crispy chicken breast

Dinner: Falafel

Day 14

Breakfast: Breakfast stuffed pastries

Lunch: Baked potatoes with broccoli

Dinner: Ranch pork chops

Day 15

Breakfast: Egg tarts

Lunch: Coconut shrimp

Dinner: Rib eye steak

Day 16

Breakfast: Breakfast biscuits

Lunch: Scallops with lemon herb sauce

Dinner: General Tso's chicken

Day 17

Breakfast: Flaxseed French toast with strawberries

Lunch: Salmon with horseradish rub

Dinner: Chicken & broccoli

Day 18

Breakfast: Breakfast peppers

Lunch: Crispy fish

Dinner: Meatballs

Day 19

Breakfast: Crispy frittata

Lunch: Fish cakes

Dinner: Lamb chops with mustard & garlic

Day 20

Breakfast: Broccoli & cheese quiche

Lunch: Crispy chicken breast

Dinner: Juicy steaks

Day 21

Breakfast: Breakfast casserole

Lunch: Sausages

Dinner: Roasted vegetables

Day 22

Breakfast: Breakfast stuffed pastries

Lunch: Brussels sprouts with bacon

Dinner: Calamari

Day 23

Breakfast: Breakfast sausage

Lunch: Salmon cakes with spicy mayo

Dinner: Mexican chicken wings

Day 24

Breakfast: Egg tarts

Lunch: Onion rings

Dinner: Lemon paprika shrimp

Day 25

Breakfast: Breakfast biscuits

Lunch: Baked potatoes

Dinner: Roast beef

Day 26

Breakfast: Crispy frittata

Lunch: Garlic & rosemary lamb chops

Dinner: Crunchy chicken tenderloins

Day 27

Breakfast: Breakfast casserole

Lunch: Ranch pork chops

Dinner: Eggplant parmesan

Day 28

Breakfast: Flaxseed French toast with strawberries

Lunch: Pork chop & Brussels sprouts

Dinner: Sausages

Day 29

Breakfast: Hash Browns

Lunch: Calamari

Dinner: Roast chicken

Day 30

Breakfast: Breakfast stuffed pastries

Lunch: Mexican chicken wings

Dinner: Lamb chops with mustard & garlic

Chapter 4: Breakfast Recipes

Hash Browns

Preparation Time: 45 minutes
Cooking Time: 20 minutes
Servings: 8

Ingredients:

- 2 teaspoons vegetable oil, divided
- 4 potatoes, grated
- 2 tablespoons corn flour
- Salt and pepper to taste
- 2 teaspoons red pepper flakes

Method:

1. Add half of oil to a pan over medium heat.
2. Cook the grated potatoes for 5 minutes, stirring often.
3. Transfer to a plate and let cool.
4. Stir in the rest of the ingredients.
5. Form patties from the mixture.
6. Refrigerate for 30 minutes.
7. Cook in the air fryer at 350 degrees F for 15 minutes, turning once.

Serving Suggestions: Serve with ketchup and mayo.

Preparation & Cooking Tips: Soak grated potatoes for 1 hour and dry thoroughly before cooking.

Breakfast Sausage

Preparation Time: 5 minutes
Cooking Time: 10 minutes
Servings: 4

Ingredients:

- 12 oz. low-fat, low-sodium sausage patties
- Cooking spray

Method:

1. Preheat your air fryer to 400 degrees F.
2. Add sausage patties to the air fryer basket.
3. Spray with oil.
4. Air fry for 5 minutes per side.

Serving Suggestions: Serve with hash browns and green salad.

Preparation & Cooking Tips: Cook in batches.

Breakfast Biscuits

Preparation Time: 15 minutes
Cooking Time: 10 minutes
Servings: 8

Ingredients:

- 2 eggs, beaten and cooked
- 4 slices turkey bacon, cooked crisp and crumbled
- 2 oz. cheddar cheese, sliced into cubes
- Pepper to taste
- 10 oz. refrigerated biscuits
- 1 egg, beaten
- 1 tablespoon water

Method:

1. In a bowl, mix the eggs, bacon, cheese and pepper.
2. Separate the refrigerate dough into 5.
3. Separate each biscuit into 2.
4. Press the biscuits to form a round shape.
5. Top with the egg mixture.
6. Place another biscuit on top and seal the edges.
7. Mix remaining egg and water.
8. Brush biscuits with this mixture.
9. Cook in the air fryer at 325 degrees F for 10 minutes.

Serving Suggestions: Serve with coffee and milk.

Preparation & Cooking Tips: You can also use pepper Jack cheese for this recipe.

Flaxseed French Toast with Strawberries

Preparation Time: 15 minutes
Cooking Time: 10 minutes
Servings: 4

Ingredients:

- ¼ cup brown sugar, divided
- ½ teaspoon ground cinnamon
- 2 eggs, beaten
- 1 teaspoon vanilla extract
- ¼ cup nonfat milk
- 4 slices whole-grain bread, sliced into strips
- 2/3 cup flax seed meal
- Cooking spray
- 1 teaspoon powdered sugar
- 2 cups strawberries, sliced

Method:

1. Add 1 tablespoon brown sugar to a bowl.
2. Stir in the cinnamon, eggs, vanilla and milk.
3. Dip the bread strips into the mixture.
4. Dredge with the flax seed meal and spray with oil.
5. Air fry at 375 degrees F for 10 minutes, turning once.
6. Add to a serving plate.
7. Sprinkle with powdered sugar.
8. Serve with strawberries on the side.

Serving Suggestions: Drizzle with honey or maple syrup.

Preparation & Cooking Tips: Choose a high-quality whole grain loaf for this recipe

Breakfast Casserole

Preparation Time: 10 minutes
Cooking Time: 25 minutes
Servings: 8

Ingredients:

- 1 teaspoon olive oil
- 1 lb. ground turkey sausage
- 1 green bell pepper, diced
- ¼ cup white onion, diced
- 8 eggs, beaten
- ½ cup Colby Jack cheese, shredded
- 1 teaspoon fennel seed
- Garlic salt to taste

Method:

1. Add oil to a pan over medium heat.
2. Cook sausage, bell pepper and onion for 10 minutes, stirring often.
3. Transfer to a bowl.
4. Stir in the remaining ingredients.
5. Transfer to a small baking pan.
6. Add to the air fryer basket.
7. Air fry at 390 degrees F for 15 minutes.

Serving Suggestions: Sprinkle with chopped green onion.

Preparation & Cooking Tips: You can also use low-sodium lean ground pork sausage.

Egg Tarts

Preparation Time: 5 minutes
Cooking Time: 20 minutes
Servings: 2

Ingredients:

- 17 oz. frozen puff pastry, sliced into 4 squares
- ¾ cup Monterey Jack cheese, shredded
- 4 eggs

Method:

1. Air fry the puff pastry at 390 degrees F for 10 minutes.
2. Press the middle part of the sheet to make indentation.
3. Sprinkle with cheese and crack eggs on top.
4. Air fry for 10 minutes.

Serving Suggestions: Sprinkle with chopped parsley.

Preparation & Cooking Tips: You can also use gruyere cheese for this recipe.

Broccoli & Cheese Quiche

Preparation Time: 20 minutes
Cooking Time: 20 minutes
Servings: 2

Ingredients:

- 2 eggs, beaten
- 1 cup low-fat milk
- 2 cups broccoli florets, steamed
- 1 cup cheddar cheese, grated
- 1 tomato, chopped
- 1 teaspoon dried thyme
- 1 teaspoon parsley, chopped
- Salt and pepper to taste

Method:

1. Combine all the ingredients in a bowl.
2. Mix well.
3. Transfer to a small baking pan.
4. Place the pan in the air fryer.
5. Cook in the air fryer at 360 degrees F for 20 minutes.

Serving Suggestions: Top with crumbled feta cheese.

Preparation & Cooking Tips: You can also use nondairy milk for this recipe.

Breakfast Peppers

Preparation Time: 10 minutes
Cooking Time: 15 minutes
Servings: 2

Ingredients:

- 2 red or green bell peppers, seeded and sliced in half
- 1 teaspoon olive oil
- 4 eggs
- Salt and pepper to taste

Method:

1. Brush the bell pepper halves with oil.
2. Crack eggs into the bell pepper halves.
3. Season with salt and pepper.
4. Add to the air fryer.
5. Cook at 330 degrees F for 15 minutes.

Serving Suggestions: Sprinkle with sriracha flakes.

Preparation & Cooking Tips: Use large bell peppers for this recipe.

Cheesy Frittata

Preparation Time: 10 minutes
Cooking Time: 20 minutes
Servings: 4

Ingredients:

- 4 eggs, beaten
- 1 green onion, chopped
- 2 tablespoons red bell pepper, diced
- ½ cup cheddar, shredded
- ¼ lb. low-sodium breakfast sausage, cooked, removed from casing and crumbled
- Pinch cayenne pepper
- Cooking spray

Method:

1. Mix all the ingredients in a bowl.
2. Preheat your air fryer to 360 degrees F.
3. Spray a small cake pan with oil.
4. Pour mixture into the pan.
5. Air fry for 20 minutes.

Serving Suggestions: Garnish with chopped parsley.

Preparation & Cooking Tips: Omit cayenne pepper if you don't want your frittata spicy.

Breakfast Stuffed Pastries

Preparation Time: 15 minutes
Cooking Time: 15 minutes
Servings: 4

Ingredients:

- 1 box puff pastry sheets, sliced into rectangles
- 5 eggs, beaten
- ½ cup turkey sausage, cooked and crumbled
- ½ cup cheddar cheese, shredded
- Cooking spray

Method:

1. Cook the eggs in a pan over medium heat.
2. Transfer to a bowl.
3. Stir in turkey sausage.
4. Top pastry sheets with egg mixture.
5. Top with cheese.
6. Add another pastry sheet on top.
7. Press to seal edges.
8. Spray with oil.
9. Air fry at 370 degrees F for 10 minutes.

Serving Suggestions: Serve with milk or coffee.

Preparation & Cooking Tips: You can also add chopped ham to the egg mixture.

Chapter 5: Chicken Recipes

Crunchy Chicken Tenderloins

Preparation Time: 10 minutes
Cooking Time: 15 minutes
Servings: 4

Ingredients:

- 1 egg, beaten
- 2 tablespoons vegetable oil
- ½ cup breadcrumbs
- 8 chicken tenderloins

Method:

1. Preheat your air fryer to 350 degrees F.
2. Add the egg to a bowl.
3. Mix the oil and breadcrumbs in another bowl.
4. Dip the chicken in egg and then in the oil mixture.
5. Add to the air fryer basket.
6. Cook for 15 minutes, flipping once or twice.

Serving Suggestions: Serve with ranch dip.

Preparation & Cooking Tips: You can also use chicken breast strips for this recipe.

Chicken & Broccoli

Preparation Time: 10 minutes
Cooking Time: 20 minutes
Servings: 4

Ingredients:

- 1 onion, sliced
- 2 cups broccoli florets
- 1 lb. chicken breast fillet, sliced into cubes
- 2 tablespoons olive oil
- ½ teaspoon garlic powder
- 1 tablespoon ginger, minced
- 1 tablespoon reduced-sodium soy sauce
- 1 teaspoon sesame seed oil
- 2 teaspoons rice vinegar

Method:

1. Toss the onion, broccoli and chicken in a bowl.
2. In another bowl, m ix the rest of the ingredients.
3. Pour mixture into the first bowl.
4. Mix well.
5. Add mixture to the air fryer.
6. Cook at 380 degrees F for 20 minutes.

Serving Suggestions: Drizzle with lemon juice before serving.

Preparation & Cooking Tips: You can also use cauliflower florets for this recipe.

Mexican Chicken Wings

Preparation Time: 10 minutes
Cooking Time: 12 minutes
Servings: 5

Ingredients:

- 3 lb. chicken wings
- 2 teaspoons olive oil
- 1 tablespoon taco seasoning mix

Method:

1. Coat chicken wings with olive oil.
2. Sprinkle all sides with taco seasoning.
3. Preheat your air fryer to 350 degrees F.
4. Add the chicken wings to the air fryer.
5. Cook for 6 minutes per side.

Serving Suggestions: Serve with salsa and sour cream.

Preparation & Cooking Tips: You can also use chicken thighs or legs for this recipe.

Crispy Chicken Breast

Preparation Time: 15 minutes
Cooking Time: 15 minutes
Servings: 2

Ingredients:

- 1 egg, beaten
- ¼ cup all-purpose flour
- ¾ cup breadcrumbs
- 1 teaspoon dried oregano
- 2 teaspoon lemon zest
- ¼ cup Parmesan cheese, grated
- Salt and pepper to taste
- ½ teaspoon cayenne pepper
- 2 chicken breast fillets

Method:

1. Add the eggs to a bowl.
2. Add the flour to another bowl.
3. In the third bowl, mix the breadcrumbs, dried oregano, lemon zest, Parmesan cheese, salt, pepper and cayenne pepper.
4. Dip the chicken breast fillets in the first, second and third bowls.
5. Add these to the air fryer basket.
6. Cook at 375 degrees F for 10 minutes.
7. Turn the chicken.
8. Cook for another 5 minutes.

Serving Suggestions: Serve with light mayo and ketchup.

Preparation & Cooking Tips: Cook for a few minutes more if you want your chicken crispier.

General Tso's Chicken

Preparation Time: 20 minutes

Cooking Time: 35 minutes

Servings: 4

Ingredients:

- 1 lb. chicken thigh fillets, sliced into smaller pieces
- Salt and pepper to taste
- 1 egg, beaten
- ¼ cup cornstarch

Sauce

- 2 tablespoons reduced sodium soy sauce
- 1 ½ tablespoons vegetable oil
- 2 teaspoons rice vinegar
- 8 tablespoons chicken broth
- 2 teaspoons sugar
- 2 tablespoons ketchup
- 3 chiles de árbol, chopped and seeded
- 1 clove garlic, minced
- 1 tablespoon ginger, chopped

Method:

1. Season chicken with salt and pepper.
2. Dip in egg and coat with cornstarch.
3. Air fry at 400 degrees F for 15 minutes, flipping once or twice.
4. In a pan over medium heat, simmer sauce ingredients for 15 minutes.
5. Add chicken to the pan.
6. Mix well.

7. Cook for 5 minutes.
8. Serve warm.

Serving Suggestions: Garnish with sesame seeds and chopped green onions.

Preparation & Cooking Tips: You can also use chicken breast fillet for this recipe.

Buttermilk Fried Chicken

Preparation Time: 8 hours and 20 minutes
Cooking Time: 45 minutes
Servings: 6

Ingredients:

Marinade

- 2 lb. chicken
- 1 cup buttermilk
- ¼ cup hot sauce
- 1 teaspoon paprika
- 1 teaspoon garlic powder
- Salt and pepper to taste

Breading

- 1 cup flour
- 1 teaspoon garlic powder
- 1 teaspoon paprika
- ½ cup cornstarch
- Salt and pepper to taste
- Cooking spray

Method:

1. Mix the marinade ingredients in a bowl.
2. Cover and refrigerate for 8 hours.
3. Preheat your air fryer to 375 degrees F.
4. In a bowl, mix the breading ingredients.
5. Add 2 tablespoons buttermilk batter to the flour bowl and mix well.
6. Dredge chicken with flour mixture.

7. Cook the chicken for 30 minutes.
8. Flip and cook for 15 minutes.

Serving Suggestions: Serve with mayo and ketchup.

Preparation & Cooking Tips: Use chicken thighs and legs for this recipe.

Parmesan Chicken

Preparation Time: 10 minutes
Cooking Time: 15 minutes
Servings: 2

Ingredients:

- 2 eggs, beaten
- 2 teaspoons paprika
- 1 ½ cups Parmesan cheese, grated
- 2 tablespoons garlic paste
- 2 tablespoons dried Italian seasoning
- 2 chicken breast fillets, sliced in half
- Salt to taste
- Cooking spray

Method:

1. Preheat your air fryer to 400 degrees F.
2. Combine paprika, cheese, garlic paste and Italian seasoning in a bowl.
3. Add the eggs to a bowl.
4. Season chicken with salt.
5. Dip in egg and then in paprika mixture.
6. Spray with oil.
7. Air fry for 15 minutes.

Serving Suggestions: Serve with roasted vegetables.

Preparation & Cooking Tips: You can also use chicken thigh fillets for this recipe.

Korean Fried Chicken

Preparation Time: 15 minutes
Cooking Time: 30 minutes
Servings: 1

Ingredients:

- 1 lb. chicken wings
- 1 tablespoon oil
- Salt and pepper to taste
- 3 tablespoons cornstarch

Sauce

- ½ tablespoon reduced-sodium soy sauce
- ½ tablespoon toasted sesame oil
- 1 tablespoon Korean chili garlic paste
- 1 tablespoon honey
- 1 tablespoon ketchup
- 1 tablespoon brown sugar
- 2 cloves garlic, minced
- ½ tablespoon ginger, grated

Method:

1. Brush chicken wings with oil.
2. Season with salt and pepper.
3. Coat with cornstarch.
4. Air fry at 400 degrees F for 15 minutes.
5. Mix sauce ingredients in a pan over medium heat.
6. Bring to a boil.
7. Reduce heat and simmer for 10 minutes.

8. Toss chicken wings in the sauce and serve.

Serving Suggestions: Garnish with white sesame seeds.

Preparation & Cooking Tips: Korean chili paste is available in most Asian stores.

Lemon Chicken

Preparation Time: 10 minutes
Cooking Time: 20 minutes
Servings: 4

Ingredients:

- 6 chicken thighs
- 2 tablespoons olive oil
- 2 tablespoons lemon juice
- 1 tablespoon Italian herb seasoning blend
- Salt and pepper to taste
- 4 lemon slices for garnish

Method:

1. Combine ingredients except garnish in a bowl.
2. Marinate for 30 minutes.
3. Place chicken in the air fryer basket.
4. Top with lemon slices.
5. Cook at 350 degrees F for 10 minutes per side.

Serving Suggestions: Drizzle with lemon juice before serving.

Preparation & Cooking Tips: You can also use chicken fillet for this recipe.

Roast Chicken

Preparation Time: 10 minutes
Cooking Time: 50 minutes
Servings: 8

Ingredients:

- 1 whole chicken
- Chicken dry rub
- Cooking spray

Method:

1. Spray chicken with oil.
2. Sprinkle with the dry rub.
3. Roast in the air fryer at 330 degrees F for 30 minutes.
4. Turn and roast for another 20 minutes.

Serving Suggestions: Serve with mashed potatoes and gravy.

Preparation & Cooking Tips: You can also use whole turkey for this recipe.

Chapter 6: Meat Recipes

Ranch Pork Chops

Preparation Time: 20 minutes
Cooking Time: 10 minutes
Servings: 4

Ingredients:

- 4 pork chops
- Cooking spray
- Garlic salt to taste
- 1 teaspoon ranch dressing mix
- Sour cream

Method:

1. Spray both sides of the pork chops with oil.
2. Sprinkle with the garlic salt and ranch dressing mix.
3. Marinate for 10 minutes.
4. Cook in the air fryer at 390 degrees F for 5 minutes per side.
5. Serve with sour cream.

Serving Suggestions: Let rest for 5 minutes before serving.

Preparation & Cooking Tips: For thicker cut pork chops, add 3 to 5 minutes of cooking time.

Rib Eye Steak

Preparation Time: 2 hours and 10 minutes
Cooking Time: 16 minutes
Servings: 2

Ingredients:

- 2 tablespoons olive oil
- ½ cup low-sodium soy sauce
- 4 teaspoons steak seasoning
- 2 rib-eye steaks, fat trimmed

Method:

1. Mix olive oil, soy sauce and steak seasoning in a bowl.
2. Add the steaks.
3. Turn to coat evenly.
4. Cover and marinate in the refrigerator for 2 hours.
5. Preheat your air fryer to 400 degrees F.
6. Air fry the steaks for 8 minutes per side.

Serving Suggestions: Let rest for 5 minutes before serving. Serve with green salad.

Preparation & Cooking Tips: Choose a cut that's one and a half inch thick.

Meatballs

Preparation Time: 20 minutes
Cooking Time: 10 minutes
Servings: 8

Ingredients:

- 16 oz. lean ground beef
- 4 oz. lean ground pork
- 1 egg, beaten
- 2 cloves garlic, minced
- ¼ cup breadcrumbs
- ½ cup Parmesan cheese, grated
- 1 teaspoon Italian seasoning
- Salt to taste

Method:

1. Preheat your air fryer to 350 degrees F.
2. Mix all the ingredients in a bowl.
3. Form meatballs from the mixture.
4. Add meatballs to the air fryer.
5. Cook for 8 minutes.
6. Shake and cook for another 2 minutes.

Serving Suggestions: Serve with marinara sauce.

Preparation & Cooking Tips: Make the meatballs ahead of time by mixing the above ingredients and freezing the meatballs for up to 1 month. Add 15 more minutes to the cooking time.

Sausages

Preparation Time: 5 minutes
Cooking Time: 10 minutes
Servings: 4

Ingredients:

- Poke the sausages in 3 places each with a sharp knife, breaking through the casing.
- Arrange the sausages in a single non-overlapping layer in the air fryer.

Method:

1. Add the sausages to the air fryer.
2. Air fry at 400 degrees F for 12 minutes.

Serving Suggestions: Serve with hot sauce and mustard.

Preparation & Cooking Tips: Poke the sausages with a fork before cooking.

Roast Beef

Preparation Time: 15 minutes
Cooking Time: 45 minutes
Servings: 6

Ingredients:

- 1 tablespoons olive oil
- 1 teaspoon thyme
- 1 teaspoon rosemary
- Salt to taste
- 2 lb. beef roast

Method:

1. Preheat your air fryer to 390 degrees F.
2. Combine olive oil, thyme, rosemary and salt in a dish.
3. Rub mixture all over the beef roast.
4. Add beef roast to the air fryer basket.
5. Cook at 360 degrees F for 15 minutes.
6. Reduce heat to 340 degrees F and cook for another 30 minutes.

Serving Suggestions: Serve with roasted vegetables.

Preparation & Cooking Tips: You can also make slits on the beef roast and insert garlic slivers.

Mustard Pork Tenderloin

Preparation Time: 4 hours and 10 minutes
Cooking Time: 20 minutes
Servings: 4

Ingredients:

- 2 tablespoons brown sugar
- ¼ cup Dijon mustard
- ½ teaspoon dried thyme
- 1 teaspoon dried parsley
- Salt and pepper to taste
- 1 ¼ lb. pork tenderloin

Method:

1. Combine all the ingredients in a bowl.
2. Cover and marinate in the refrigerator for 4 hours.
3. Preheat your air fryer to 400 degrees F.
4. Air fry the pork for 20 minutes.

Serving Suggestions: Serve with roasted green beans or potatoes.

Preparation & Cooking Tips: You can also marinate the night before.

Pork Chops & Brussels Sprouts

Preparation Time: 15 minutes
Cooking Time: 15 minutes
Servings: 2

Ingredients:

- 2 pork chops
- Cooking spray
- Salt and pepper to taste
- 2 teaspoons olive oil
- 2 cups Brussels sprouts
- 1 teaspoon mustard
- 2 teaspoons maple syrup

Method:

1. Spray both sides of pork chops with oil.
2. Season with salt and pepper.
3. In a bowl, mix the remaining ingredients.
4. Add the pork chops to one side of the air fryer.
5. Place the Brussels sprouts on the other side.
6. Cook at 400 degrees F for 15 minutes.

Serving Suggestions: Drizzle with maple syrup before serving.

Preparation & Cooking Tips: If available, use Dijon mustard for this recipe.

Garlic & Rosemary Lamb Chops

Preparation Time: 10 minutes

Cooking Time: 15 minutes

Servings: 2

Ingredients:

- 4 lamb chops
- 2 teaspoons olive oil
- Salt and pepper to taste
- 1 clove garlic, minced
- 2 tablespoons rosemary, chopped

Method:

1. Brush lamb chops with oil.
2. Season with salt and pepper.
3. Place in the air fryer basket.
4. Top with garlic and rosemary.
5. Cook at 360 degrees F and cook for 6 to 8 minutes per side.

Serving Suggestions: Garnish with lemon wedges.

Preparation & Cooking Tips: You can also let lamb chops marinate in the garlic and rosemary for 30 minutes.

Juicy Steaks

Preparation Time: 20 minutes
Cooking Time: 12 minutes
Servings: 2

Ingredients:

- 2 rib eye steaks
- Salt and pepper to taste
- 2 tablespoons olive oil

Garlic butter sauce

- ½ cup butter (unsalted), softened
- 1 teaspoon Worcestershire Sauce
- 2 teaspoons garlic, minced
- 2 tablespoons parsley, chopped
- Salt to taste

Method:

1. Combine the garlic butter sauce ingredients in a bowl.
2. Form a log from the mixture.
3. Wrap with foil and refrigerate.
4. Coat steaks with olive oil.
5. Sprinkle both sides with salt and pepper.
6. Cook in the air fryer at 400 degrees F for 6 minutes per side.
7. Add garlic butter on top.

Serving Suggestions: Serve with green salad.

Preparation & Cooking Tips: Let steaks rest for 20 minutes before coating with olive oil and seasoning.

Lamb Chops with Mustard & Garlic

Preparation Time: 45 minutes
Cooking Time: 20 minutes
Servings: 2

Ingredients:

Marinade

- 1 teaspoon garlic, minced
- 2 teaspoons olive oil
- 2 teaspoons Dijon mustard
- 1 teaspoon soy sauce
- 1 teaspoon cayenne pepper
- 1 teaspoon cumin powder
- Salt to taste

Lamb

- 8 lamb chops

Method:

1. Combine the marinade ingredients in a bowl.
2. Add the lamb chops.
3. Cover and marinate for 30 minutes.
4. Add to the air fryer basket.
5. Air fry at 350 degrees F for 20 minutes, flipping once or twice.

Serving Suggestions: Sprinkle with cumin before serving.

Preparation & Cooking Tips: For thicker lamb chops, add 3 to 5 minutes of cooking time.

Chapter 7: Fish & Seafood Recipes

Scallops with Lemon Herb Sauce

Preparation Time: 10 minutes
Cooking Time: 6 minutes
Servings: 2

Ingredients:

- Cooking spray
- 8 scallops
- Salt and pepper to taste
- ¼ cup olive oil
- ½ teaspoon garlic, chopped
- 1 teaspoon lemon zest
- 2 teaspoons capers, minced
- 2 tablespoons parsley, chopped

Method:

1. Spray your air fryer basket with oil.
2. Season scallops with salt and pepper.
3. Air fry scallops at 400 degrees F for 6 minutes.
4. In a bowl, mix the oil, garlic, lemon zest, capers and parsley.
5. Pour sauce over the scallops and serve.

Serving Suggestions: Garnish with lemon wedges.

Preparation & Cooking Tips: Dry scallops thoroughly before seasoning.

Sesame Cod & Snap Peas

Preparation Time: 10 minutes
Cooking Time: 20 minutes
Servings: 4

Ingredients:

- Cooking spray
- 4 cod fillets
- Salt and pepper to taste
- 3 tablespoons butter, melted
- 2 tablespoons sesame seeds
- Vegetable oil
- 3 cloves garlic, sliced thinly
- 12 oz. sugar snap peas
- 1 orange, sliced into wedges

Method:

1. Preheat it to 400 degrees F.
2. Sprinkle both sides of fish with salt and pepper.
3. In a bowl, mix sesame seeds and butter.
4. Reserve 2 tablespoons of this mixture.
5. Toss garlic and peas in the butter mixture.
6. Air fry for 10 minutes, shaking once.
7. Brush both sides of fish with reserved butter mixture.
8. Cook for 5 minutes per side.
9. Serve fish with snap peas and garlic.

Serving Suggestions: Garnish with orange wedges.

Preparation & Cooking Tips: You can also toast sesame seeds first before mixing with butter.

Coconut Shrimp

Preparation Time: 10 minutes
Cooking Time: 6 minutes
Servings: 6

Ingredients:

- Pepper to taste
- ½ cup all-purpose flour
- 2 eggs
- ¼ cup breadcrumbs
- ⅔ cup coconut flakes (unsweetened)
- 12 oz. shrimp, peeled and deveined
- Cooking spray
- Salt to taste
- ¼ cup lime juice
- ¼ cup honey
- 1 Serrano chili, chopped

Method:

1. Mix pepper and flour in a bowl.
2. Add the eggs to another bowl.
3. In a third bowl, combine breadcrumbs and coconut flakes.
4. Coat shrimp with flour.
5. Dip in eggs and dredge with breadcrumbs.
6. Spray with oil.
7. Cook in the air fryer for 3 minutes per side.
8. Season with salt.
9. In a bowl, mix the remaining ingredients.
10. Serve shrimp with lime honey dip.

Serving Suggestions: Garnish with chopped cilantro.

Preparation & Cooking Tips: Replace Serrano chili with 2 teaspoons red pepper flakes if not available.

Calamari

Preparation Time: 10 minutes
Cooking Time: 4 minutes
Servings: 4

Ingredients:

- ½ cup all-purpose flour
- 1 egg
- ¼ cup milk
- Salt and pepper to taste
- 2 cups breadcrumbs
- 1 lb. calamari rings
- Cooking spray

Method:

1. Preheat your air fryer to 400 degrees F.
2. Add flour to a bowl.
3. Beat egg and milk in another bowl.
4. Mix salt, pepper and breadcrumbs in a third bowl.
5. Coat calamari with flour.
6. Dip in egg.
7. Dredge with breadcrumb mixture.
8. Air fry calamari for 4 minutes.
9. Flip and cook for another 3 minutes.

Serving Suggestions: Serve with cocktail sauce.

Preparation & Cooking Tips: Freeze breaded calamari and air fry when ready to cook.

Crispy Fish

Preparation Time: 10 minutes
Cooking Time: 15 minutes
Servings: 4

Ingredients:

- ¼ cup vegetable oil
- 1 cup breadcrumbs
- 4 flounder fillets
- 1 egg, beaten

Method:

1. Preheat your air fryer to 350 degrees F.
2. Combine oil and breadcrumbs in a bowl.
3. Soak the fish in the egg.
4. Coat with the breadcrumb mixture.
5. Add to the air fryer basket.
6. Air fry for 15 minutes, turning once.

Serving Suggestions: Garnish with lemon slices.

Preparation & Cooking Tips: You can also use other white fish fillet for this recipe.

Garlic Popcorn Shrimp

Preparation Time: 15 minutes
Cooking Time: 8 minutes
Servings: 4

Ingredients:

- Cooking spray
- ½ cup all-purpose flour
- 2 tablespoons water
- 2 eggs, beaten
- 1 tablespoon garlic powder
- 1 tablespoon ground cumin
- 1 ½ cups breadcrumbs
- 1 lb. shrimp, peeled and deveined

Dipping sauce

- ½ cup ketchup
- 2 tablespoons lime juice
- 2 tablespoons fresh cilantro leaves, chopped
- 2 tablespoons chipotle chili in adobo, chopped
- Salt to taste

Method:

1. Spray your air fryer basket with oil.
2. Add flour to a dish.
3. In a bowl, mix water and eggs.
4. In another bowl, combine garlic powder, cumin and breadcrumbs.
5. Coat shrimp with flour.
6. Dip shrimp in egg and dredge with garlic powder mixture.

7. Spray with oil.
8. Air fry at 360 degrees F for 8 minutes, flipping once.
9. Mix the remaining ingredients.
10. Serve shrimp with dipping sauce.

Serving Suggestions: Garnish with lime wedges.

Preparation & Cooking Tips: Use freshly squeezed lime juice.

Salmon with Horseradish Rub

Preparation Time: 10 minutes
Cooking Time: 15 minutes
Servings: 2

Ingredients:

- Cooking spray
- 1 tablespoon olive oil
- 2 tablespoons horseradish, grated
- 1 tablespoon capers, chopped
- 1 tablespoon parsley, chopped
- 2 salmon fillets
- Salt and pepper to taste

Method:

1. Spray your air fryer basket with oil.
2. Mix oil, horseradish, capers and parsley in a bowl.
3. Season salmon with salt and pepper.
4. Spread horseradish mixture on top of salmon.
5. Air fry at 375 degrees F for 15 minutes.

Serving Suggestions: Let rest for 5 minutes before serving.

Preparation & Cooking Tips: Spray salmon with oil after spreading it with horseradish mixture.

Lemon Paprika Shrimp

Preparation Time: 10 minutes
Cooking Time: 10 minutes
Servings: 2

Ingredients:

- 1 tablespoon olive oil
- 1 tablespoon lemon juice
- 1 teaspoon lemon pepper
- ¼ teaspoon paprika
- ¼ teaspoon garlic powder
- 12 Oz. shrimp, peeled and deveined

Method:

1. Preheat your air fryer to 400 degrees F.
2. Combine all the ingredients in a bowl.
3. Coat shrimp evenly with the sauce mixture.
4. Add shrimp to the air fryer.
5. Cook for 8 to 10 minutes.

Serving Suggestions: Garnish with lemon slices.

Preparation & Cooking Tips: You can also use frozen peeled shrimp.

Salmon Cakes with Spicy Mayo

Preparation Time: 45 minutes
Cooking Time: 10 minutes
Servings: 4

Ingredients:

Spicy mayo

- ¼ cup mayonnaise
- 1 tablespoon hot sauce

Salmon cakes

- 1 lb. salmon fillets, chopped
- 1 egg, beaten
- ¼ cup almond flour
- 1 green onion, chopped
- 1 ½ teaspoon Old Bay seasoning
- Cooking spray

Method:

1. Mix spicy mayo ingredients.
2. Refrigerate until ready to use.
3. Combine salmon cake ingredients in a bowl.
4. Form patties from the mixture.
5. Refrigerate patties for 30 minutes.
6. Air fry the salmon cakes at 390 degrees F for 4 to 5 minutes per side.
7. Serve with spicy mayo mixture.

Serving Suggestions: Garnish with chopped green onion.

Preparation & Cooking Tips: Cook in batches.

Fish Cakes

Preparation Time: 10 minutes
Cooking Time: 20 minutes
Servings: 2

Ingredients:

- Cooking spray
- 10 oz. cod fillet, chopped
- 3 tablespoons cilantro, chopped
- ¼ cup breadcrumbs
- ¼ cup breadcrumbs
- 1 egg, beaten
- 2 tablespoons light mayonnaise
- 2 tablespoons Thai sweet chili sauce
- Salt and pepper to taste

Method:

1. Spray air fryer basket with oil.
2. Combine all ingredients in a bowl.
3. Form patties from the mixture.
4. Spray patties with oil.
5. Add to the air fryer basket.
6. Air fry at 400 degrees F for 10 minutes, flipping once.

Serving Suggestions: Garnish with chopped cilantro.

Preparation & Cooking Tips: Make fish cakes ahead of time by freezing the mixture and air frying the frozen fish cakes when ready to serve.

Chapter 8: Vegetarian Recipes

Eggplant Parmesan

Preparation Time: 15 minutes
Cooking Time: 17 minutes
Servings: 4

Ingredients:

Breading

- ½ cup breadcrumbs
- ½ teaspoon onion powder
- ½ teaspoon garlic powder
- 1 teaspoon Italian seasoning
- ½ teaspoon dried basil
- ¼ cup Parmesan cheese, grated
- Salt and pepper to taste

Eggplant

- ¼ cup flour
- 2 eggs, beaten
- 1 eggplant, sliced into rounds
- 1 cup reduced-sodium marinara sauce
- 8 slices low-sodium mozzarella cheese

Method:

1. Mix breading ingredients in a bowl.
2. Add flour to another bowl and eggs to a third bowl.
3. Coat eggplant with flour.
4. Dip in egg.

5. Dredge with breading mixture.
6. Preheat your air fryer to 370 degrees F.
7. Add eggplant to the air fryer basket.
8. Cook for 10 minutes.
9. Flip and cook for another 5 minutes.
10. Top with marinara sauce and cheese.
11. Cook for another 2 minutes.

Serving Suggestions: Garnish with chopped parsley.

Preparation & Cooking Tips: Let eggplant rest for 5 minutes before air frying.

Falafel

Preparation Time: 10 minutes
Cooking Time: 12 minutes
Servings: 4

Ingredients:

- 1 cup chickpeas
- ¼ cup onion, chopped
- 2 cloves garlic, minced
- ½ cup parsley, chopped
- 1 tablespoon olive oil
- 1 tablespoon lemon juice
- 1 tablespoon water
- ¼ teaspoon baking soda
- 1 tablespoon ground cumin
- Salt to taste

Method:

1. Add all the ingredients to a food processor.
2. Process until finely chopped.
3. Form patties from the mixture.
4. Spray your air fryer basket with oil.
5. Add patties to the air fryer basket.
6. Air fry at 375 degrees F for 6 minutes per side.

Serving Suggestions: Serve with toasted bread or cooked brown rice.

Preparation & Cooking Tips: You can use dried chickpeas but soak these overnight first.

Brussels Sprouts with Bacon

Preparation Time: 5 minutes
Cooking Time: 30 minutes
Servings: 8

Ingredients:

- 4 slices bacon
- 1 onion, chopped
- 3 lb. Brussels sprouts, sliced in half
- 1 tablespoon olive oil
- Salt and pepper to taste
- 2 teaspoons thyme
- 2 tablespoons lemon juice

Method:

1. Add bacon to the air fryer.
2. Air fry at 400 degrees F for 15 minutes, turning once.
3. Drain on a plate lined with paper towel.
4. Let cool and then crumble.
5. Coat onion and Brussels sprouts with oil.
6. Season with salt and pepper.
7. Cook in the air fryer at 375 degrees F for 15 minutes, shaking the basket once.
8. Top Brussels sprouts with bacon, thyme and lemon juice.

Serving Suggestions: Garnish with lemon wedges.

Preparation & Cooking Tips: Use center-cut bacon for this recipe if possible.

Baked Potatoes with Broccoli

Preparation Time: 15 minutes
Cooking Time: 25 minutes
Servings: 8

Ingredients:

- 4 potatoes
- 1 cup low-fat milk, divided
- 2 tablespoons all-purpose flour
- ½ cup Cheddar cheese, shredded and divided
- 1 cup broccoli florets, chopped
- Salt and pepper to taste

Method:

1. Poke potatoes with a fork.
2. Microwave on high for 10 minutes.
3. Transfer to a cutting board and slice in half.
4. In a pan over medium heat, simmer ¾ cup low-fat milk.
5. In a bowl, mix remaining milk and flour.
6. Add this to the pan.
7. Bring to a boil.
8. Turn off heat.
9. Add cheese, broccoli, salt and pepper to the pan.
10. Add the potatoes to the air fryer basket.
11. Top with the cheese mixture.
12. Air fry at 350 degrees F for 5 minutes.

Serving Suggestions: Garnish with chopped chives.

Preparation & Cooking Tips: You may also add a pinch of cayenne pepper to the mixture.

Roasted Okra

Preparation Time: 5 minutes
Cooking Time: 12 minutes
Servings: 2

Ingredients:

- 1 lb. okra, trimmed
- 1 teaspoon olive oil
- Garlic powder to taste
- Salt and pepper to taste

Method:

1. Preheat your air fryer to 350 degrees F.
2. Toss okra in oil.
3. Season with garlic powder, salt and pepper.
4. Add to the air fryer.
5. Air fry okra for 5 minutes.
6. Shake and cook for another 5 minutes.
7. Shake once more and cook for 2 minutes.

Serving Suggestions: Drizzle with a little vinegar before serving.

Preparation & Cooking Tips: You can also use garlic salt in place of garlic powder and salt.

Crispy Green Tomatoes

Preparation Time: 15 minutes
Cooking Time: 15 minutes
Servings: 6

Ingredients:

- 2 green tomatoes, sliced
- Salt and pepper to taste
- ¼ cup all purpose flour
- 2 eggs, beaten
- ½ cup buttermilk
- 1 cup breadcrumbs
- ½ teaspoon paprika
- 1 teaspoon garlic powder
- 1 cup yellow cornmeal
- 1 tablespoon olive oil

Method:

1. Sprinkle tomato with salt and pepper.
2. Add flour to a bowl.
3. Mix eggs and milk to a second bowl.
4. Combine the remaining ingredients except oil to a third bowl.
5. Coat tomatoes with flour.
6. Dip in egg and cover with breadcrumb mixture.
7. Add tomatoes to the air fryer basket.
8. Drizzle with oil.
9. Cook for 12 minutes.
10. Flip and cook for another 3 minutes.

Serving Suggestions: Serve with spicy mayo.

Preparation & Cooking Tips: Cook the tomatoes in batches.

Onion Rings

Preparation Time: 15 minutes
Cooking Time: 5 minutes
Servings: 4

Ingredients:

- ¾ cup all-purpose flour
- Salt to taste
- 2 teaspoons baking powder
- ½ cup cornstarch
- 1 large white onion, sliced into rings
- 1 cup milk
- 1 egg, beaten
- 1 cup bread crumbs
- Cooking spray
- Garlic powder to taste

Method:

1. Combine flour, salt, baking powder and cornstarch in a bowl.
2. Coat onion rings with the mixture.
3. Beat egg and milk in another bowl.
4. Dip onion rings in egg mixture.
5. Dredge with breadcrumbs.
6. Preheat your air fryer to 400 degrees F.
7. Add to the air fryer basket.
8. Spray with oil
9. Cook onion rings for 3 to 5 minutes, flipping once.
10. Sprinkle with garlic powder before serving.

Serving Suggestions: Serve with dip of choice.

Preparation & Cooking Tips: You can also season with paprika.

Spicy Green Beans

Preparation Time: 20 minutes
Cooking Time: 12 minutes
Servings: 4

Ingredients:

- 12 oz. green beans, trimmed
- 1 clove garlic, minced
- 1 teaspoon soy sauce
- 1 teaspoon rice wine vinegar
- 1 tablespoon sesame oil
- ½ teaspoon crushed red pepper

Method:

1. Preheat your air fryer to 400 degrees F.
2. Add green beans to a bowl.
3. Stir in the remaining ingredients.
4. Marinate for 5 minutes.
5. Air fry for 12 minutes, shaking once or twice.

Serving Suggestions: Serve with garlic mayo dip.

Preparation & Cooking Tips: You can marinate longer for 15 minutes.

Baked Potatoes

Preparation Time: 15 minutes

Cooking Time: 1 hour

Servings: 2

Ingredients:

- 2 potatoes
- 1 tablespoon peanut oil
- Salt to taste

Method:

1. Preheat your air fryer to 400 degrees F.
2. Coat potatoes with peanut oil.
3. Season with salt.
4. Add to the air fryer basket.
5. Air fry for 1 hour.

Serving Suggestions: Serve with sour cream or cheese sauce.

Preparation & Cooking Tips: Poke with a fork to see if the potatoes are done.

Roasted Vegetables

Preparation Time: 20 minutes
Cooking Time: 10 minutes
Servings: 4

Ingredients:

- 1 red bell pepper, sliced
- 1 squash, diced
- ½ cup zucchini, diced
- 1 cup cauliflower florets
- 1 cup mushrooms, diced
- 2 teaspoons vegetable oil
- Salt and pepper to taste

Method:

1. Preheat your air fryer to 360 degrees F.
2. Combine all the ingredients in a bowl.
3. Transfer to the air fryer basket.
4. Air fry for 10 minutes, shaking once or twice.

Serving Suggestions: Adjust seasoning before serving.

Preparation & Cooking Tips: You can also add other vegetables like carrots and potatoes.

Chapter 9: Snack Recipes

Fish & Chips

Preparation Time: 20 minutes
Cooking Time: 20 minutes
Servings: 4

Ingredients:

- 2 potatoes, sliced into wedges
- Cooking spray
- Salt to taste
- 1 cup all purpose flour
- 2 eggs, beaten
- 2 tablespoons water
- 1 cup breadcrumbs
- 4 white fish fillets, sliced into strips
- Cooking spray

Method:

1. Add potato wedges to the air fryer basket.
2. Air fry at 375 degrees F for 10 minutes, turning once.
3. Season potato wedges with salt.
4. In a bowl, mix water and eggs.
5. Coat fish fillet strips with flour.
6. Dip in egg mixture, and dredge with breadcrumbs.
7. Spray with oil.
8. Add to the air fryer basket.
9. Cook at 375 degrees F for 10 minutes, flipping once.
10. Serve fish with potato wedges.

Serving Suggestions: Serve with mayo and ketchup.

Preparation & Cooking Tips: Cook in batches.

Spicy Potato Wedges

Preparation Time: 15 minutes
Cooking Time: 15 minutes
Servings: 4

Ingredients:

- 2 potatoes, sliced into wedges
- 1 ½ tablespoons olive oil
- ½ teaspoon chili powder
- ½ teaspoon parsley flakes
- ½ teaspoon paprika
- Salt and pepper to taste

Method:

1. Preheat your air fryer to 400 degrees F.
2. Toss potatoes in oil.
3. Sprinkle with chili powder, parsley flakes, paprika, salt and pepper.
4. Air fry for 10 minutes.
5. Flip and cook for another 5 minutes.

Serving Suggestions: Serve with ketchup and light mayo.

Preparation & Cooking Tips: Soak potatoes in cold water before air frying but be sure to dry thoroughly with paper towels.

Curried Chickpeas

Preparation Time: 10 minutes
Cooking Time: 15 minutes
Servings: 4

Ingredients:

- 15 oz. unsalted chickpeas, rinsed, drained and skinned
- 2 tablespoons olive oil
- 2 tablespoons red wine vinegar
- Salt to taste
- ¼ teaspoon ground cinnamon
- ½ teaspoon ground turmeric
- 2 teaspoons curry powder
- ¼ teaspoon ground cumin
- ¼ teaspoon ground coriander
- Pinch Aleppo pepper

Method:

1. Toss chickpeas in oil and vinegar.
2. Sprinkle with salt and spices.
3. Add to the air fryer basket.
4. Cook at 400 degrees F for 15 minutes, shaking once halfway through.

Serving Suggestions: Garnish with chopped cilantro.

Preparation & Cooking Tips: You can use red pepper flakes instead of Aleppo pepper.

Sesame Kale Chips

Preparation Time: 5 minutes
Cooking Time: 6 minutes
Servings: 2

Ingredients:

- 6 cups kale leaves
- ½ teaspoon garlic, minced
- 1 teaspoon white sesame seeds
- ¼ teaspoon poppy seeds
- 1 teaspoon soy sauce

Method:

1. Combine all the ingredients in a bowl.
2. Add to the air fryer basket.
3. Cook at 375 degrees F for 6 minutes, shaking once.

Serving Suggestions: Serve immediately.

Preparation & Cooking Tips: Dry leaves thoroughly before seasoning.

Cinnamon Plantain Chips

Preparation Time: 10 minutes
Cooking Time: 10 minutes
Servings: 2

Ingredients:

- 1 plantain, sliced thinly
- Avocado oil spray
- Cinnamon powder to taste

Method:

1. Preheat your air fryer to 350 degrees F.
2. Spray chips with oil.
3. Air fry for 7 minutes.
4. Flip and cook for another 3 minutes.
5. Sprinkle with cinnamon powder.

Serving Suggestions: Sprinkle with a little salt before serving.

Preparation & Cooking Tips: Use green plantain for best results.

Potato Chips

Preparation Time: 15 minutes
Cooking Time: 30 minutes
Servings: 4

Ingredients:

- 1 potato, sliced into rounds
- 1 tablespoon oil
- 1 teaspoon rosemary, chopped

Method:

1. Coat potato rounds with oil.
2. Air fry at 375 degrees F for 30 minutes.
3. Sprinkle with rosemary.

Serving Suggestions: Sprinkle with a little salt before serving.

Preparation & Cooking Tips: Potato slices should be 1/8 inch thick.

Greek Feta Fries

Preparation Time: 15 minutes
Cooking Time: 15 minutes
Servings: 2

Ingredients:

- Cooking spray

Fries

- 2 potatoes, sliced into strips
- 1 tablespoon olive oil
- ½ teaspoon dried oregano
- 2 teaspoons lemon zest
- ¼ teaspoon garlic powder
- ¼ teaspoon onion powder
- ¼ teaspoon paprika
- Salt and pepper to taste

Toppings

- 2 oz. chicken breast, cooked and shredded
- 2 oz. feta cheese, grated
- 2 tablespoons red onion, chopped
- ¼ cup tomato, chopped
- 1 tablespoon parsley, chopped
- ¼ cup tzatziki

Method:

1. Preheat your air fryer to 380 degrees F.
2. Spray your air fryer basket with oil.

3. Coat potatoes with olive oil.
4. Season with herbs, spices and salt.
5. Air fry for 15 minutes, flipping once or twice.
6. Transfer to a serving plate.
7. Add remaining ingredients on top.

Serving Suggestions: Serve with sour cream.

Preparation & Cooking Tips: Soak potatoes in cold water for 30 minutes and dry thoroughly before air frying.

Zucchini Chips

Preparation Time: 15 minutes
Cooking Time: 10 minutes
Servings: 8

Ingredients:

- 2 zucchinis, sliced into rounds
- ½ cup cornstarch
- 4 egg whites
- 2 cups breadcrumbs
- Cooking spray
- Salt to taste

Dip

- ½ cup mayonnaise
- 1 cup sour cream
- 2 teaspoons fresh dill, chopped
- 2 tablespoons chives, chopped
- 2 teaspoons lemon juice

Method:

1. Coat zucchini with cornstarch.
2. Dip in egg whites.
3. Dredge with breadcrumbs.
4. Spray zucchini with oil.
5. Air fry at 400 degrees F for 5 minutes.
6. Flip and cook for another 5 minutes.
7. Transfer to a plate.
8. Season with salt.
9. Mix the dip ingredients.
10. Serve with the zucchini chips.

Serving Suggestions: Garnish with fresh dill.

Preparation & Cooking Tips: Use freshly squeezed lemon juice.

Pickle Chips

Preparation Time: 10 minutes
Cooking Time: 6 minutes
Servings: 4

Ingredients:

- 16 oz. pickle chips
- ½ cup all purpose flour
- 2 eggs, beaten
- 1 cup breadcrumbs

Dip

- 1 tablespoon mustard
- ¼ cup mayonnaise
- ½ teaspoon smoked paprika
- 1 teaspoon lemon juice

Method:

1. Cover pickle chips with flour.
2. Dip in eggs and dredge with breadcrumbs.
3. Add to the air fryer basket.
4. Air fry at 350 degrees F for 6 minutes.
5. Mix the dip ingredients.
6. Serve pickle chips with dip.

Serving Suggestions: Serve immediately.

Preparation & Cooking Tips: Use Creole mustard if available.

Roasted Peanuts

Preparation Time: 10 minutes
Cooking Time: 20 minutes
Servings: 8

Ingredients:

- 8 oz. peanuts
- 2 tablespoons olive oil
- ½ teaspoon cayenne pepper
- 3 teaspoons Old Bay seasoning
- Salt to taste

Method:

1. Preheat your air fryer to 320 degrees F.
2. Toss peanuts in olive oil.
3. Season with cayenne pepper, Old Bay seasoning and salt.
4. Place peanuts in the air fryer basket.
5. Cook for 10 minutes.
6. Shake the basket and cook for another 10 minutes.

Serving Suggestions: Drain peanuts after cooking.

Preparation & Cooking Tips: You can also add more cayenne pepper if you like the peanuts spicier.

Chapter 10: Appetizer Recipes

Buffalo Wings

Preparation Time: 20 minutes
Cooking Time: 40 minutes
Servings: 4

Ingredients:

- 4 lb. chicken wings
- ½ teaspoon onion powder
- ½ teaspoon garlic powder
- 1 ½ teaspoons paprika
- Pepper to taste
- 2 tablespoons butter (unsalted)
- ½ cup Buffalo sauce
- ¼ cup ranch dressing

Method:

1. Preheat your oven to 200 degrees F.
2. Preheat your air fryer to 375 degrees F.
3. Season chicken wings with onion powder, garlic powder, paprika and pepper.
4. Marinate for 10 minutes.
5. Add to the air fryer.
6. Air fry for 15 minutes.
7. Flip and cook for another 10 minutes.
8. In a pan over medium heat, mix butter and Buffalo sauce.
9. Simmer for 5 minutes.
10. Toss chicken wings in sauce.
11. Transfer to a baking pan.
12. Bake in the oven for 10 minutes.

Serving Suggestions: Serve with carrot and celery sticks.

Preparation & Cooking Tips: You can also use hot sauce instead of Buffalo sauce.

Stuffed Peppers

Preparation Time: 10 minutes
Cooking Time: 10 minutes
Servings: 3

Ingredients:

- 12 oz. ground turkey, cooked
- ¾ cup reduced-sodium marinara sauce
- ¼ cup breadcrumbs
- ½ cup brown rice, cooked
- ¼ cup Parmesan cheese, grated
- Pepper to taste
- 3 tablespoons parsley, chopped
- 3 large red bell peppers, tops sliced off

Method:

1. Mix all the ingredients except bell peppers in a bowl.
2. Stuff mixture into the bell peppers.
3. Cook in the air fryer at 350 degrees F for 10 minutes.

Serving Suggestions: Garnish with chopped chives.

Preparation & Cooking Tips: You can omit rice for low-carb meal.

Egg Rolls

Preparation Time: 20 minutes
Cooking Time: 10 minutes
Servings: 4

Ingredients:

- 5 oz. lean ground pork
- ¼ cup scallions, chopped
- 3 cups cabbage, sliced
- 2 cloves garlic, minced
- 1 teaspoon reduced-sodium soy sauce
- 1 tablespoon lime juice
- 1 egg, beaten
- 6 egg roll wrappers
- Cooking spray

Method:

1. Add all ingredients except wrappers to a bowl.
2. Mix well.
3. Top wrappers with the mixture.
4. Roll up the wrappers and seal.
5. Spray with oil.
6. Air fry at 390 degrees F for 5 minutes per side.

Serving Suggestions: Serve with sweet chili sauce.

Preparation & Cooking Tips: Freeze egg rolls and air fry when ready to serve.

Mac & Cheese Balls

Preparation Time: 20 minutes
Cooking Time: 12 minutes
Servings: 4

Ingredients:

- 7 oz. mac and cheese mix (low-sodium), cooked according to package directions
- ¼ cup milk
- 2 tablespoons butter
- ¾ cup cheddar cheese, shredded
- Cooking spray
- Salt to taste
- Pinch garlic powder
- 2 eggs, beaten
- 1 cup breadcrumbs

Method:

1. Preheat your air fryer to 350 degrees F.
2. Mix mac and cheese, milk, butter and cheese in a bowl.
3. Form balls from the mixture.
4. Sprinkle with salt and garlic powder.
5. Dip in eggs and dredge with breadcrumbs.
6. Cook for 8 minutes.
7. Turn and cook for another 4 minutes.

Serving Suggestions: Serve with ketchup.

Preparation & Cooking Tips: Freeze mac and cheese balls and air fry when ready to serve.

Pork Dumplings

Preparation Time: 20 minutes
Cooking Time: 12 minutes
Servings: 6

Ingredients:

Dumplings

- 4 oz. lean ground pork
- 3 cloves garlic, minced
- 1 tablespoon ginger, chopped
- ¼ teaspoon red pepper flakes
- 1 tablespoon scallions, chopped
- 18 wonton wrappers

Sauce

- 2 teaspoons reduced-sodium soy sauce
- 2 tablespoons rice vinegar
- ½ teaspoon brown sugar
- 1 teaspoon sesame oil

Method:

1. Combine dumpling ingredients except wrappers in a bowl.
2. Mix well.
3. Add mixture on top of wrappers.
4. Fold wrappers and seal.
5. Add to the air fryer basket.
6. Air fry at 375 degrees F for 12 minutes.
7. Mix sauce ingredients.
8. Serve dumplings with sauce.

Serving Suggestions: Garnish with chopped chives.

Preparation & Cooking Tips: Cook in batches.

Jalapeño Poppers

Preparation Time: 15 minutes
Cooking Time: 10 minutes
Servings: 4

Ingredients:

- ¼ cup scallion, chopped
- ¼ cup chicken breast, cooked and chopped
- 1 oz. cheddar cheese, shredded
- 2 oz. cream cheese, softened
- 2 teaspoons fresh dill, chopped
- 2 tablespoons hot sauce
- 2 tablespoons breadcrumbs
- 4 jalapeño peppers, sliced in half
- Cooking spray

Method:

1. Mix all the ingredients except jalapeño peppers in a bowl.
2. Top jalapeño peppers with the mixture.
3. Spray with oil.
4. Place in the air fryer basket.
5. Air fry at 370 degrees F for 10 minutes.

Serving Suggestions: Serve with hot sauce.

Preparation & Cooking Tips: You can also use red bell peppers for this recipe.

Scallops with Bacon

Preparation Time: 15 minutes

Cooking Time: 10 minutes

Servings: 8

Ingredients:

Spicy Mayo

- ½ cup mayonnaise
- 2 tablespoons hot pepper sauce

Scallops

- 1 lb. scallops
- Salt and pepper to taste
- 12 to 15 slices turkey bacon
- Cooking spray

Method:

1. Combine mayo and hot sauce in a bowl. Set aside.
2. Preheat your air fryer to 390 degrees F.
3. Season scallops with salt and pepper.
4. Wrap with turkey bacon.
5. Secure with toothpicks.
6. Spray with oil.
7. Air fry scallops for 7 minutes.
8. Turn and cook for 3 minutes.
9. Serve with spicy mayo.

Serving Suggestions: Garnish with chopped chives.

Preparation & Cooking Tips: Dry scallops thoroughly before seasoning with salt and pepper.

Peppers Stuffed with Sausage

Preparation Time: 10 minutes
Cooking Time: 5 minutes
Servings: 20

Ingredients:

- 1 clove garlic, minced
- 8 oz. Italian sausage, removed from casing, cooked and crumbled
- 2 tablespoons blue cheese, crumbled
- ½ cup cheddar cheese, shredded
- 8 oz. cream cheese
- 2 tablespoons breadcrumbs
- Pepper to taste
- 16 oz. large sweet peppers, tops sliced off

Method:

1. Preheat your air fryer to 350 degrees F.
2. Mix garlic, sausage, cheeses, breadcrumbs and peppers in a bowl.
3. Stuff peppers with the mixture.
4. Air fry for 5 minutes.

Serving Suggestions: Garnish with chopped chives.

Preparation & Cooking Tips: You can also use chicken or turkey sausage for this recipe.

Tofu Bites

Preparation Time: 15 minutes
Cooking Time: 15 minutes
Servings: 20

Ingredients:

- 8 oz. tofu, sliced into cubes
- 4 tablespoons cornstarch
- 4 tablespoons rice milk (unsweetened)
- ⅛ teaspoon paprika
- ⅛ teaspoon onion powder
- ⅛ teaspoon garlic powder
- Pepper to taste
- ¾ cup breadcrumbs

Method:

1. Coat tofu cubes with cornstarch.
2. Dip in egg.
3. Mix the remaining ingredients.
4. Dredge tofu cubes with breadcrumb mixture.
5. Air fry tofu cubes at 375 degrees F for 15 minutes, flipping twice.

Serving Suggestions: Serve with Buffalo sauce.

Preparation & Cooking Tips: Freeze tofu first and then thaw before slicing and cooking.

Sausage Bites

Preparation Time: 15 minutes
Cooking Time: 20 minutes
Servings: 6

Ingredients:

- ⅛ teaspoon ground allspice
- ½ teaspoon ground turmeric
- 3 tablespoons honey
- ½ cup beer
- ½ cup mustard
- 6 sausages, sliced
- 6 sweet peppers, seeded

Method:

1. Add allspice, turmeric, honey and beer to a pan over medium heat.
2. Bring to a boil.
3. Reduce heat and simmer for 10 minutes.
4. Turn off heat and add mustard.
5. Add sausages and sweet peppers in the air fryer basket.
6. Cook at 400 degrees F for 10 minutes.
7. Serve with mustard sauce.

Serving Suggestions: Garnish with chopped chives.

Preparation & Cooking Tips: Use spicy mustard.

Chapter 10: Side Dish Recipes

Roasted Cauliflower & Broccoli

Preparation Time: 15 minutes
Cooking Time: 15 minutes
Servings: 4

Ingredients:

- 2 cups cauliflower florets
- 2 cups broccoli florets
- 1 tablespoon peanut oil
- 3 cloves garlic, minced
- ½ teaspoon paprika
- Salt to taste

Method:

1. Preheat your air fryer to 400 degrees F.
2. Coat the cauliflower and broccoli in oil.
3. Sprinkle with garlic, paprika and salt.
4. Transfer to the air fryer.
5. Cook for 15 minutes, turning every 5 minutes.

Serving Suggestions: Serve with dip of choice.

Preparation & Cooking Tips: You can also use olive oil instead of peanut oil.

Cauliflower Gnocchi

Preparation Time: 10 minutes
Cooking Time: 10 minutes
Servings: 8

Ingredients:

- 20 oz. frozen cauliflower gnocchi
- 3 tablespoons olive oil
- ½ cup Parmesan cheese, grated

Method:

1. Preheat your air fryer to 375 degrees F.
2. Toss gnocchi in the oil and sprinkle with Parmesan cheese.
3. Add to the air fryer basket.
4. Air fry for 5 minutes.
5. Shake and cook for another 5 minutes.

Serving Suggestions: Serve with marinara sauce.

Preparation & Cooking Tips: You can also use this recipe for other types of gnocchi.

Orange & Sesame Tofu

Preparation Time: 10 minutes
Cooking Time: 15 minutes
Servings: 4

Ingredients:

- 28 oz. tofu, sliced into cubes
- Cooking spray
- ¼ cup orange juice
- 2 tablespoons reduced-sodium soy sauce
- 1 tablespoon honey
- 1 teaspoon sesame oil

Method:

1. Air fry tofu cubes at 375 degrees F for 15 minutes, flipping once.
2. In a pan over medium heat, simmer the remaining ingredients for 15 minutes.
3. Toss tofu in the orange sesame sauce before serving.

Serving Suggestions: Garnish with chopped scallions.

Preparation & Cooking Tips: Dry tofu before air frying.

Garlic Baby Potatoes

Preparation Time: 10 minutes
Cooking Time: 20 minutes
Servings: 4

Ingredients:

- 1 lb. baby potatoes, sliced in half
- 1 tablespoon avocado oil
- ½ teaspoon granulated garlic
- ½ teaspoon dried parsley flakes
- Salt to taste

Method:

1. Preheat your air fryer to 350 degrees F.
2. Toss the potatoes in oil.
3. Season with garlic, parsley and salt.
4. Cook in the air fryer for 20 minutes, shaking once or twice.

Serving Suggestions: Sprinkle with Parmesan cheese.

Preparation & Cooking Tips: Replace dried parsley with chopped fresh parsley.

Roasted Butternut Squash

Preparation Time: 10 minutes
Cooking Time: 12 minutes
Servings: 6

Ingredients:

- 2 butternut squash, sliced into cubes
- 2 tablespoons avocado oil
- 2 tablespoons thyme, chopped
- Salt to taste

Method:

1. Toss the squash cubes in oil.
2. Sprinkle with thyme and salt.
3. Add to the air fryer.
4. Cook at 380 degrees F for 12 minutes, turning once.

Serving Suggestions: Drizzle with honey.

Preparation & Cooking Tips: You can also use rosemary instead of thyme.

Conclusion

If you desire for a healthy body, but you don't know how to match the ingredients and what to make food with. Then the Low Sodium Meal Prep Cookbook for Beginners is perfect for you. Follow this cookbook with straightforward instructions, encouraging advice, and time-saving tips make meal planning. And stick to it and you'll make a big difference.

www.ingramcontent.com/pod-product-compliance
Lightning Source LLC
Chambersburg PA
CBHW081403070526
44583CB00020B/2650